A Note for Parents + Teachers

This workbook will help your student understand musical notation beyond the common 5-finger pattern reading. Please note that this workbook is intended to be a supplement in addition to other method books. While this book does not contain pieces to be played, the exercises will help your student understand the graphical representation of notes so they can more easily read music and get those fingers moving!

Parents- the more you understand, the better you can help! I encourage you to practice these exercises along with your child to better your own understanding.

Teachers- feel free to expand on the ideas outlined in these pages to best suit the needs of your individual students.

Thank you for joining me in this musical study!

-Alec Sloane

Pitch and Rhythm

Pitch and Rhythm are the two most important aspects of music.

Pitch is how high or low a note sounds and Rhythm is the placement of the notes.

It is helpful to think of these two parts of music as going along the sides of a graph:

Pitch will go up and down. Rhythm will go left to right.

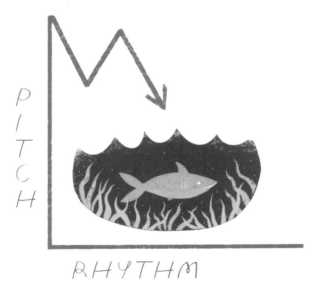

The notes in this song go down to the sea!

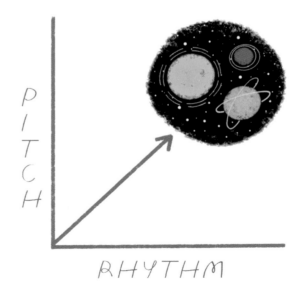

The notes in this song go up into outer space!

Counting the Beats

Rhythm is the location of the notes being played on a grid of beats.
Think of the notes as spaces in a grid that move left to right

1 - 2 - 3 - 4

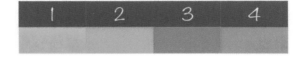

Now, keep the same steady beat but skip some numbers

1 - - 3 - 4

Even when there's no note, the beat is still there.
Keeping the beat steady is the most important part about rhythm.

Count out loud and clap where the grids are colored in.

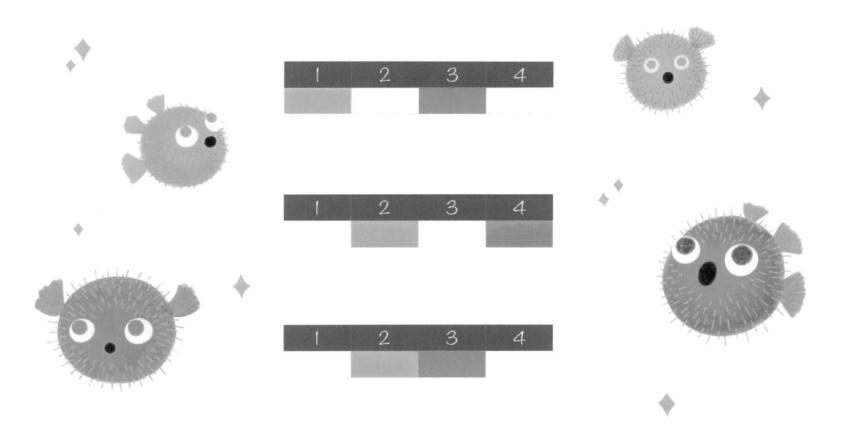

Different Types of Notes

Different types of notes make different types of rhythms.
The way a note is written represents how long or short the note will be played.

Each note gets a partner rest.
The rests represent beats where a note is not played.

Note		Rest	
○	Whole	▬	The longest note is the WHOLE NOTE The whole note and rest are 4 beats long
𝅗𝅥	Half	▬	Half of the whole note is the HALF NOTE The half note and rest are 2 beats long
𝅘𝅥	Quarter	𝄽	Half of the half note is the QUARTER NOTE The quarter note and rest are 1 beat long
𝅘𝅥𝅮	Eighth	𝄾	Half of the quarter note is the EIGHTH NOTE The eighth note and rest are half of 1 beat

What types of notes do the spaces in the grids need?

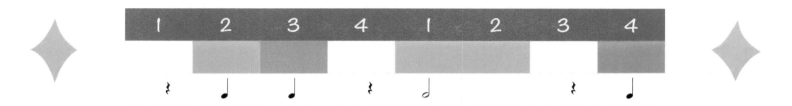

Remember, beats that don't have notes still need rests!

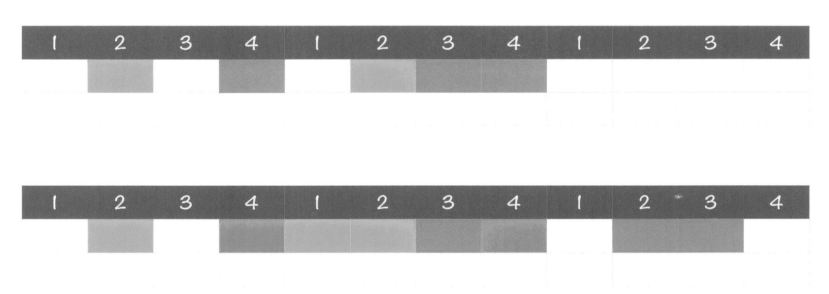

Great work!

The Musical Alphabet

Pitch represents how high and how low notes are in music.

Pitch can be seen vertically on the staff and can be thought of as the "up-and-down" part of music reading.

We organize musical pitch by using the Musical Alphabet!

When the melody goes up, we use the letter A-G:

A - B - C - D - E - F - G - A - B - C - D - E - F - G

When the melody goes down, the notes are played backwards:

G - F - E - D - C - B - A - G - F - E - D - C - B - A

Combining Pitch and Rhythm

The chart below represents different notes at different times.
Keep a steady beat while saying the note names out loud.

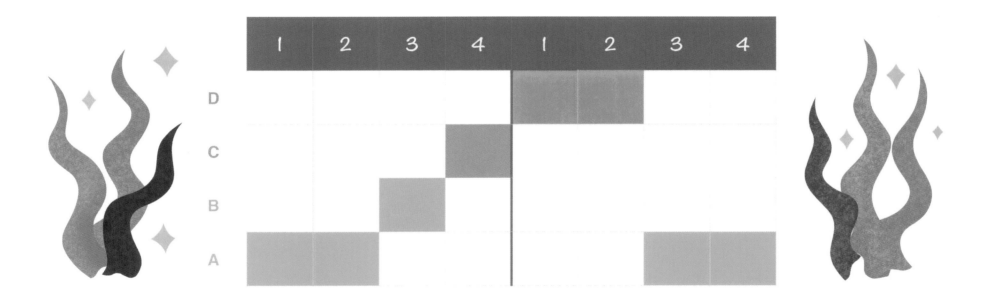

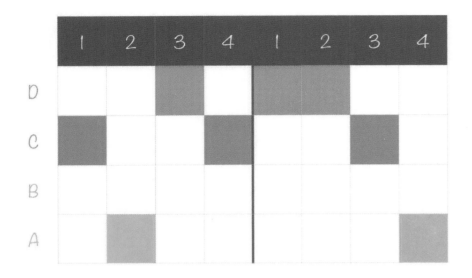

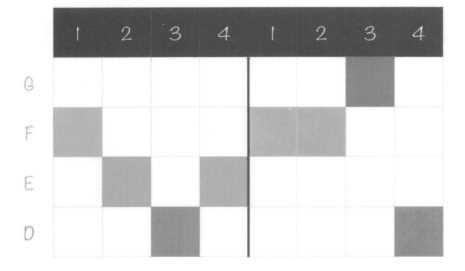

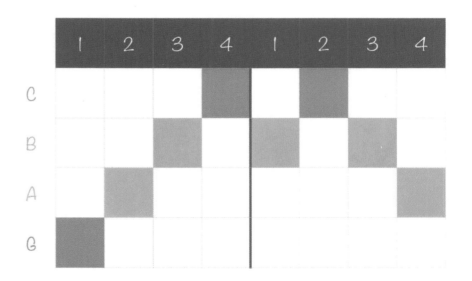

8.

Reading the Staff

A long time ago, musicians invented the Staff. At its heart the staff is only five lines and four spaces. Don't be fooled though, the staff is a very powerful tool!

Notes can be placed on the lines or in the spaces of the staff to indicate how high or low they are, and also how far apart they are from each other.

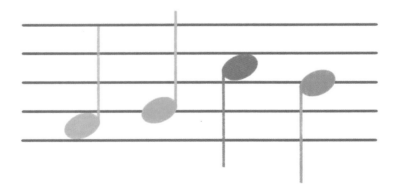

For example, the first two notes on the staff are right next to each other, and the second is higher than the first.
The third note leaps up, skipping over two notes, and the fourth note is a step down.

Understanding Clefs

The Clefs are used to give each staff a reference pitch.

The Treble Clef is drawn around the G note on the staff
and represents notes played on the right side of the keyboard:

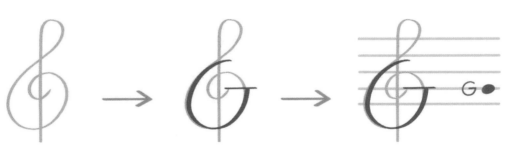

The Bass Clef is drawn around the F note on the staff
and represents notes played on the left side of the keyboard:

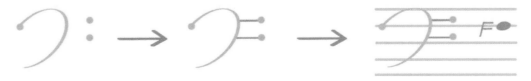

Because the "G" note lies on the 2nd line of the staff,

The notes in the spaces of the Treble Clef are F - A - C - E

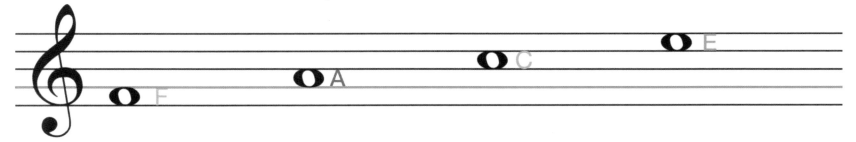

Because the "F" note lies on the 4th line of the staff,

The notes in the spaces of the Bass Clef are A - C - E - G

Translate the rhythm grids into notes on the staff.

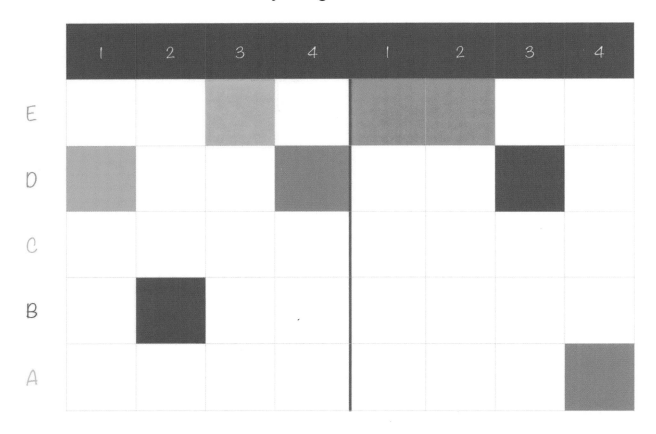

Remember, every note has a rhythm value as well as a pitch!

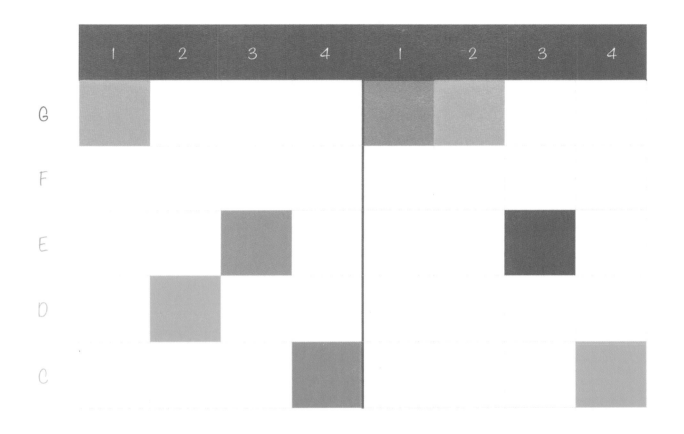

13.

Now try a few the other way around! Translate these notes onto our rhythm grids.

	1	2	3	4	1	2	3	4
G								
F								
E								
D								
C								

Notes on the Piano

The keyboard is broken up by groups of 2 and 3 black keys.

Use this trick to remember the location of a couple of the white keys:

The letter C has 2 ends, so it goes with a group of 2 black keys.
The Letter F has 3 ends, so it goes with a group of 3 black keys.

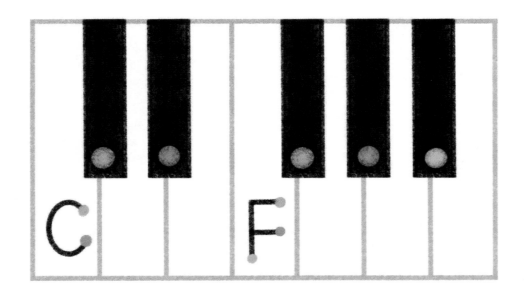

Try to fill in all the letter names for the white keys below with the musical alphabet:

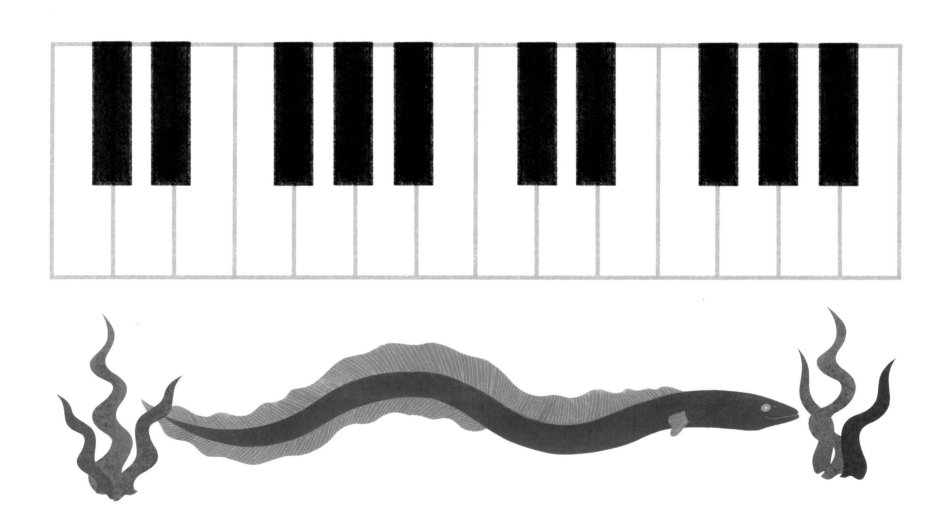

Time Signatures

A Time Signature is a pair of numbers at the beginning of a piece of music.
Time Signatures represent how to break up the rhythm of each measure.
It's helpful to think of these beats as boxes:

The top number represents how many beats (or boxes) there are per measure.

The bottom number represents what type of note will fill each box.

To better understand Time Signatures, visualize the measures broken up into rhythm grids:

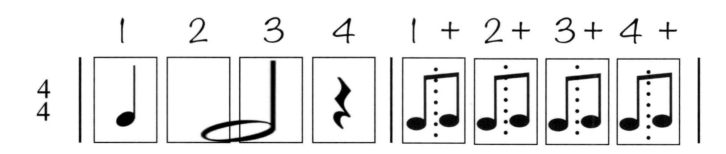

Since the eighth notes are only half a beat, these notes are usually paired together to make one beat.
Counting 1 + 2 + also shows that these notes belong to the same beat.

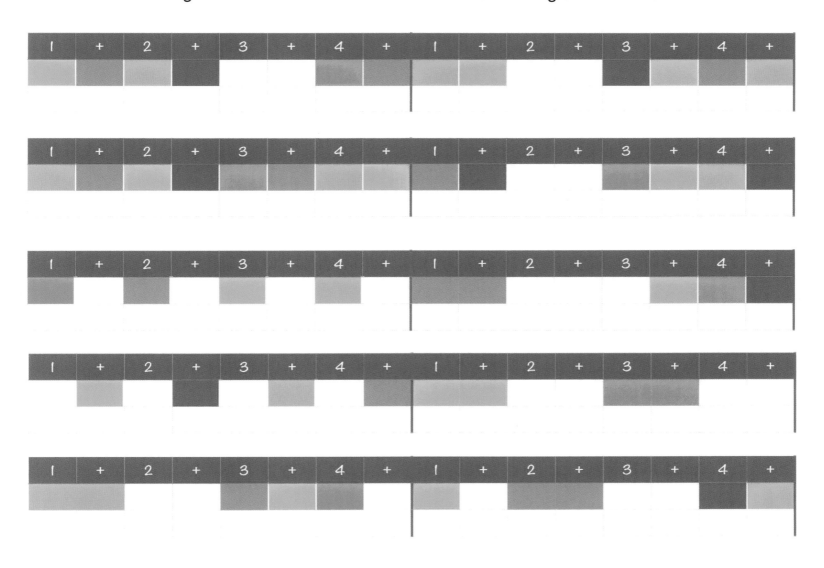

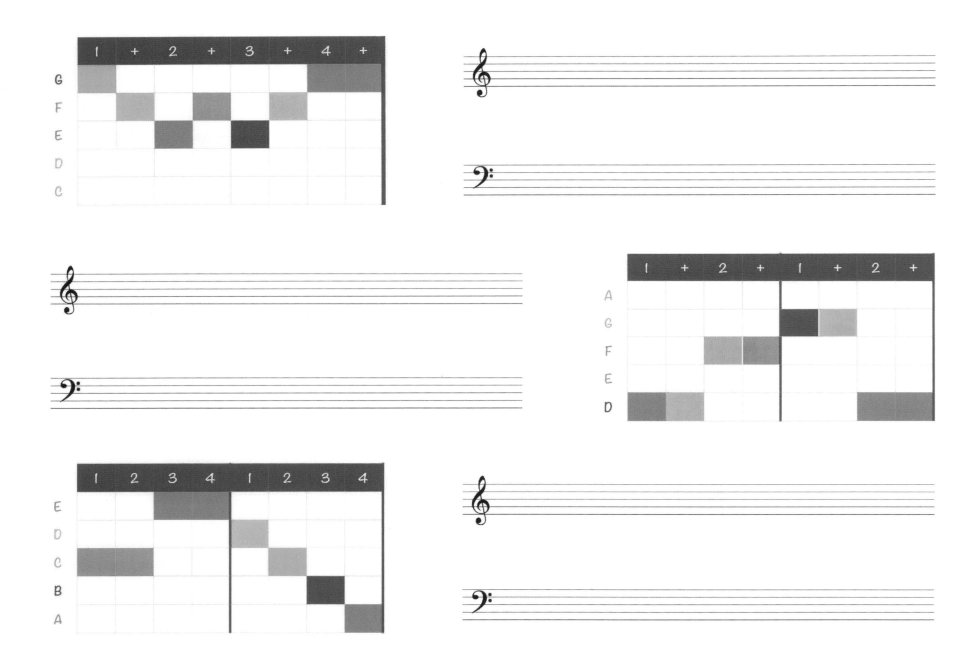

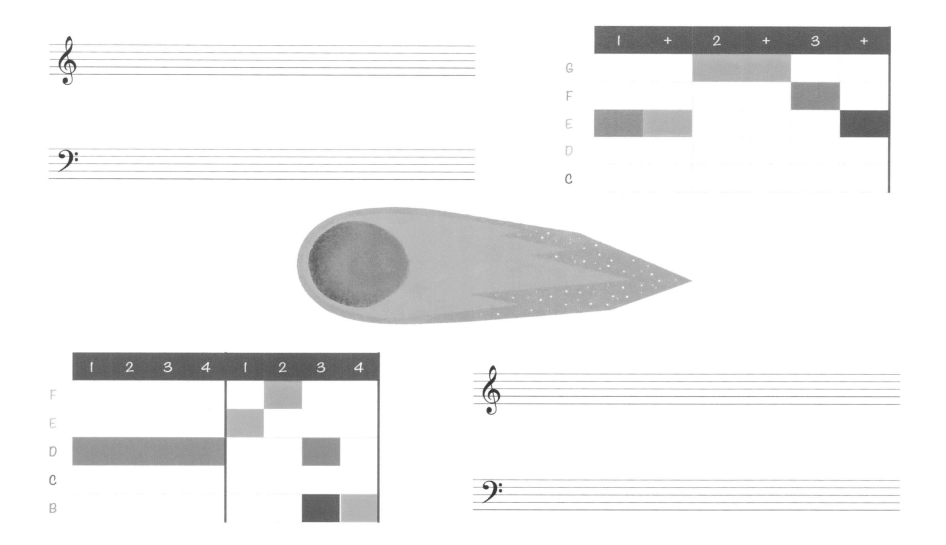

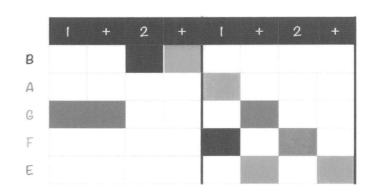

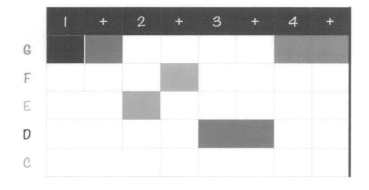

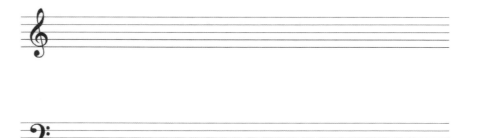

22.

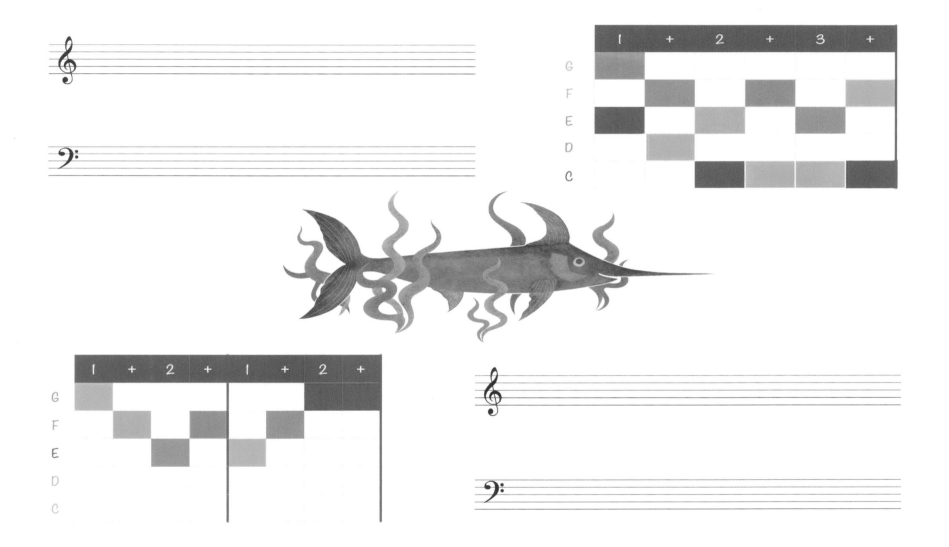

Alright! Now let's try a few the other way around.
I'll leave a couple blank at the end so you can try some more on your own!

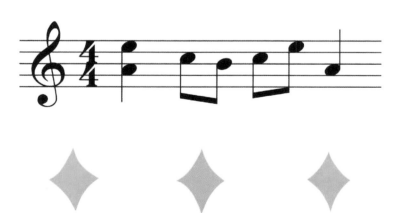

25.

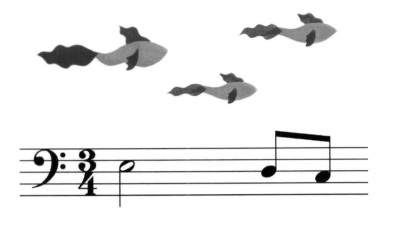

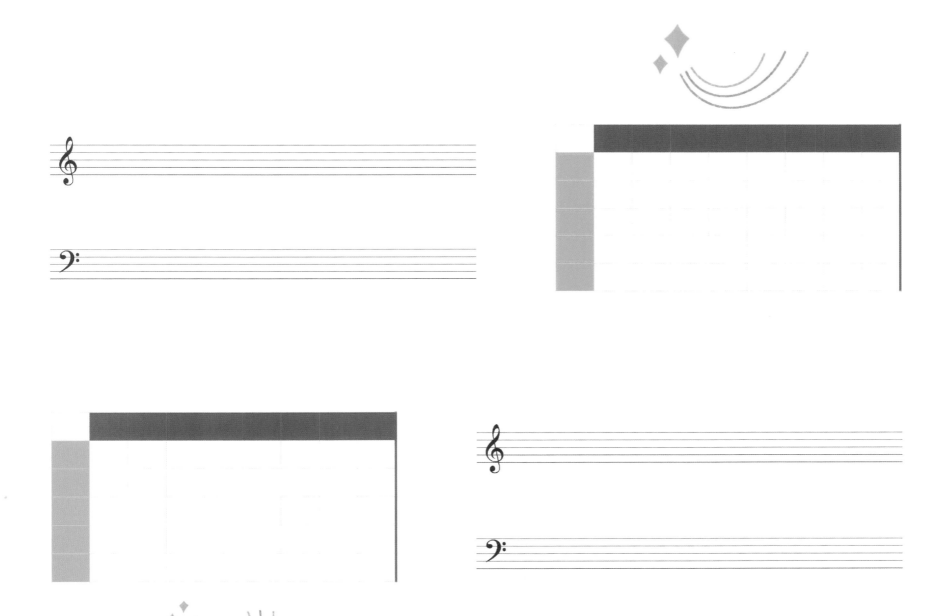

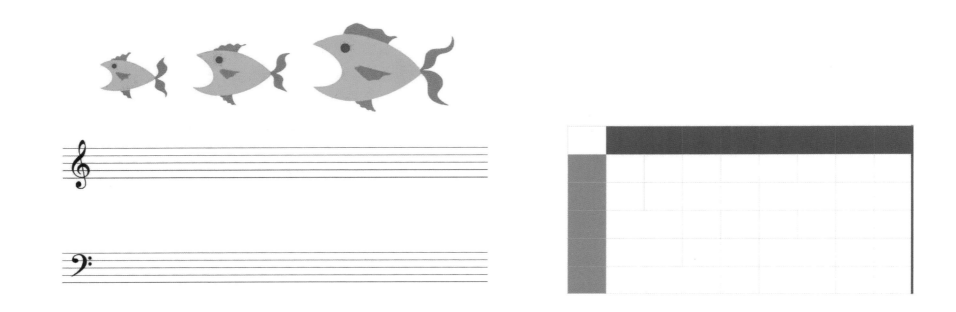

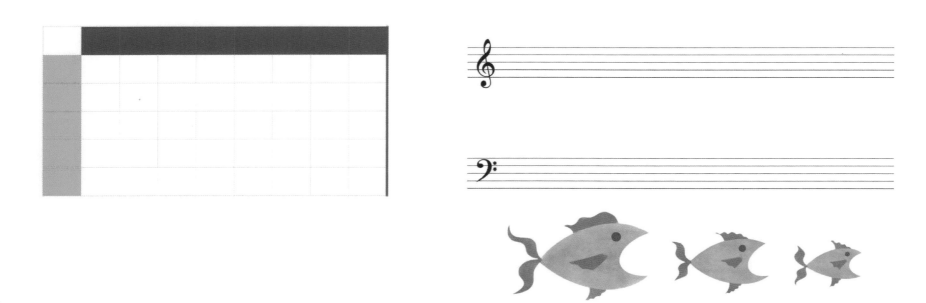

28.

Great Work!! You're ready to start reading on your own!
I can't wait to hear what you play!

About the Author

Alec Sloane is a composer and educator from Northern California. He developed the method of reading seen in this workbook during his years of teaching at Pleasanton Academy of Music in Pleasanton, California. He would like to extend his thanks to the support of the Academy in making this book possible.

Since graduating from University of the Pacific's Conservatory of Music, he has taught in both private and group settings; covering Music Theory, Composition, Guitar, Piano, and Voice. Because of his background in popular music, Alec is very familiar with the struggles many young students face when trying to learn the more disciplined notation style of classical Piano.

CPSIA information can be obtained at www.ICGtesting.com
Printed in the USA
LVIW011625111020
668356LV00003BA/52